The Bible Coloring Book

Glen R. Landin

CREATIVEARTISTIC PUBLISHING

ORANGE, CALIFORNIA

ISBN-10: 0996280731

ISBN-13: 978-0996280730

PRINTED EDITION: JANUARY 2016

PRINTED IN THE UNITED STATES OF AMERICA

WWW.GLENLANDIN.COM

WWW.CREATIVEARTISTICPUBLISHING.COM

Holy Bible

HOLY BIBLE

BELIEVE ON THE LORD JESUS CHRIST,
AND YOU WILL BE SAVED
ACTS 16:31

IN THE BEGINNING, GOD CREATED THE HEAVENS AND THE EARTH
GENESIS 1:1

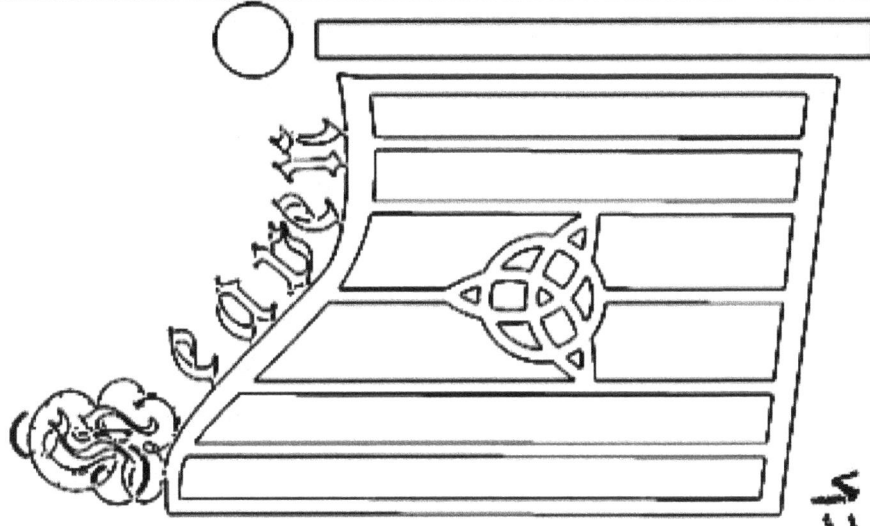

Faith

Heaven & Earth

Jesus Christ

BE STILL, AND KNOW THAT I AM GOD
PSALM 46:10

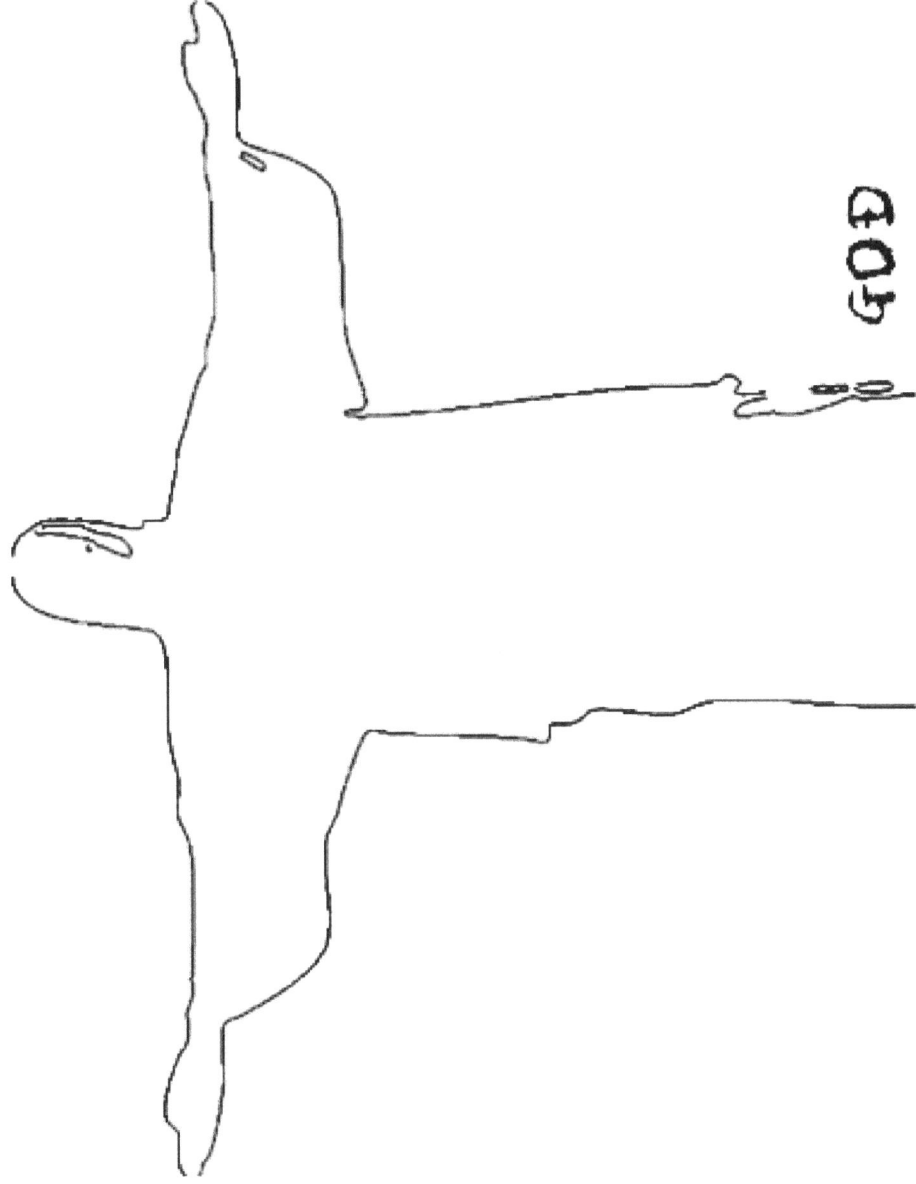

GOD

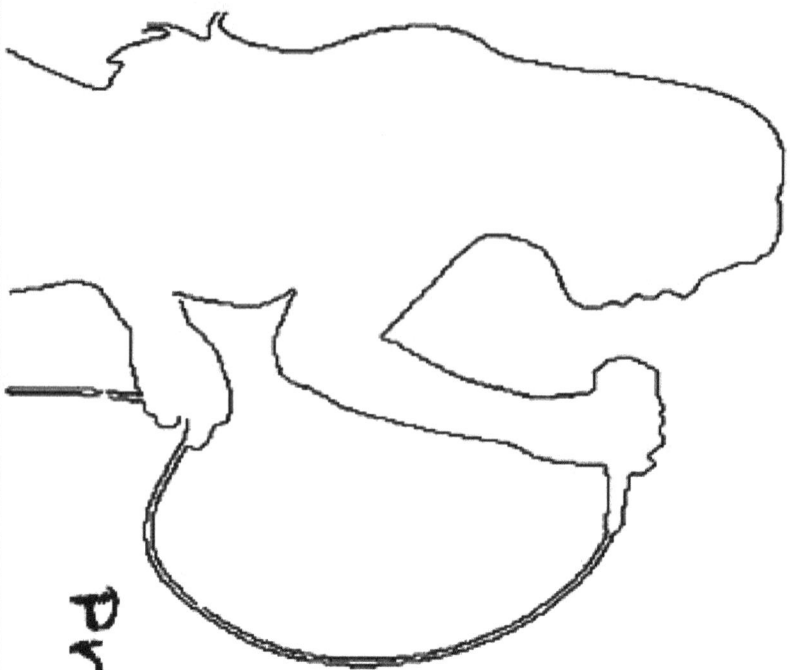

Praising

EACH ONE MUST GIVE AS HE HAS
DECIDED IN HIS HEART....
2 CORINTHIANS 9:7

Offerings & Tithes

I CAN DO EVERYTHING THROUGH HIM
WHO GIVES ME STRENGTH
PHILIPPIANS 4:13

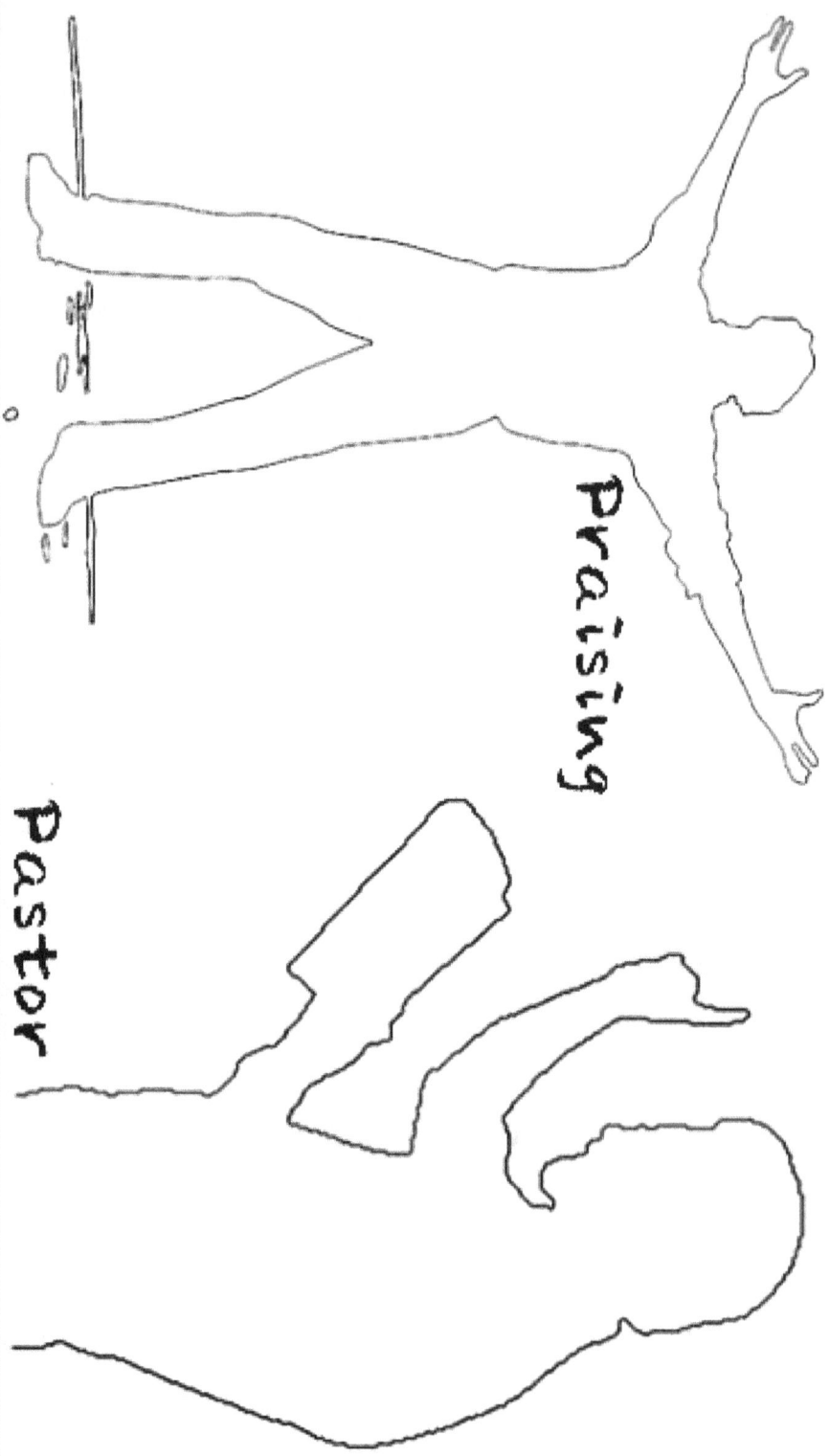

Praising

Pastor

REJOICE IN THE LORD ALWAYS.
I WILL SAY IT AGAIN: REJOICE!
PHILIPPIANS 4:4

Angels Rejoice

I PRAISE YOU GOD, FOR I AM
FEARFULLY AND WONDERFULLY MADE
PSALM 139:14

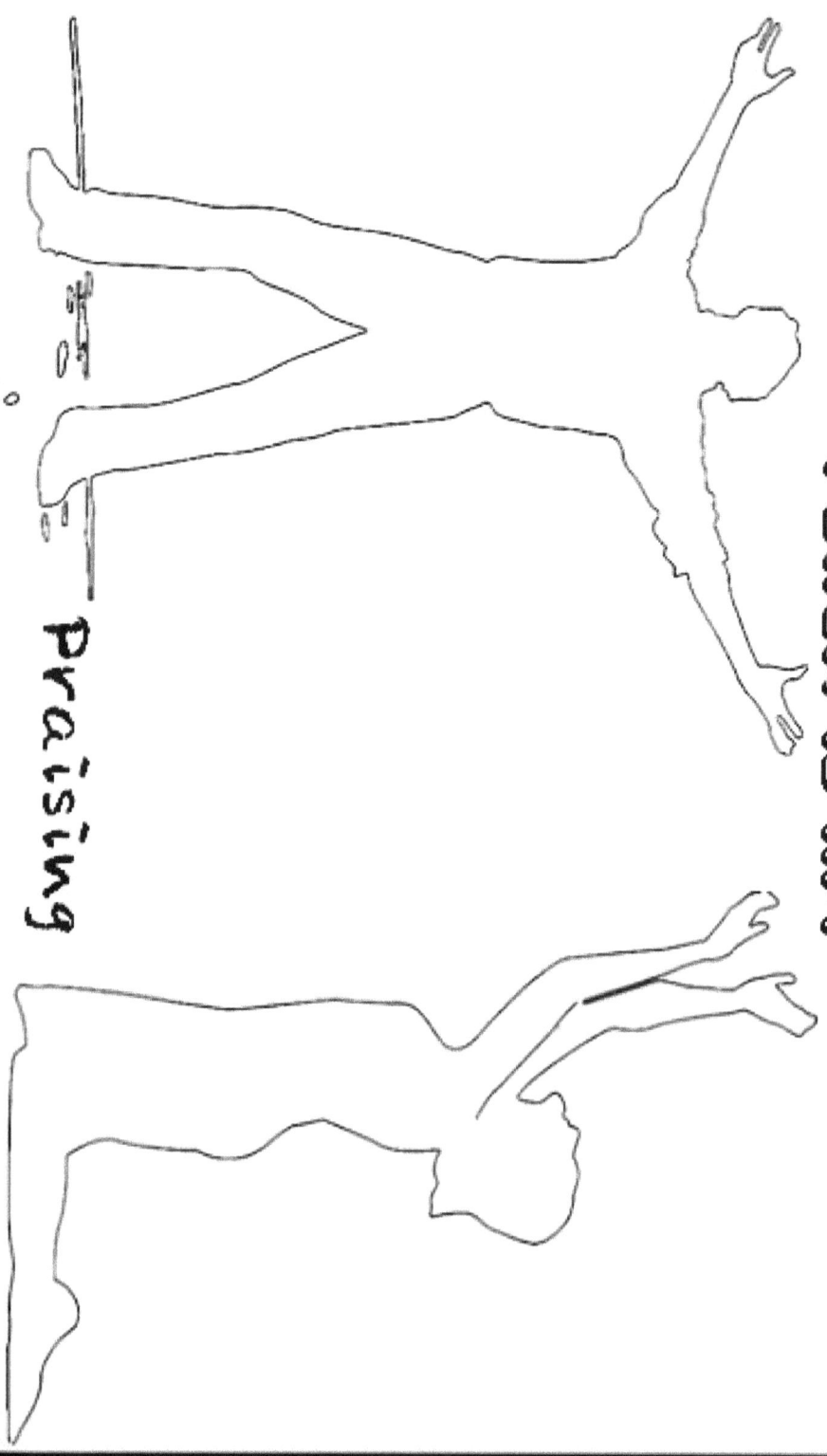

Praising

ARE NOT TWO SPARROWS SOLD FOR A PENNY?... MATTHEW 10:24

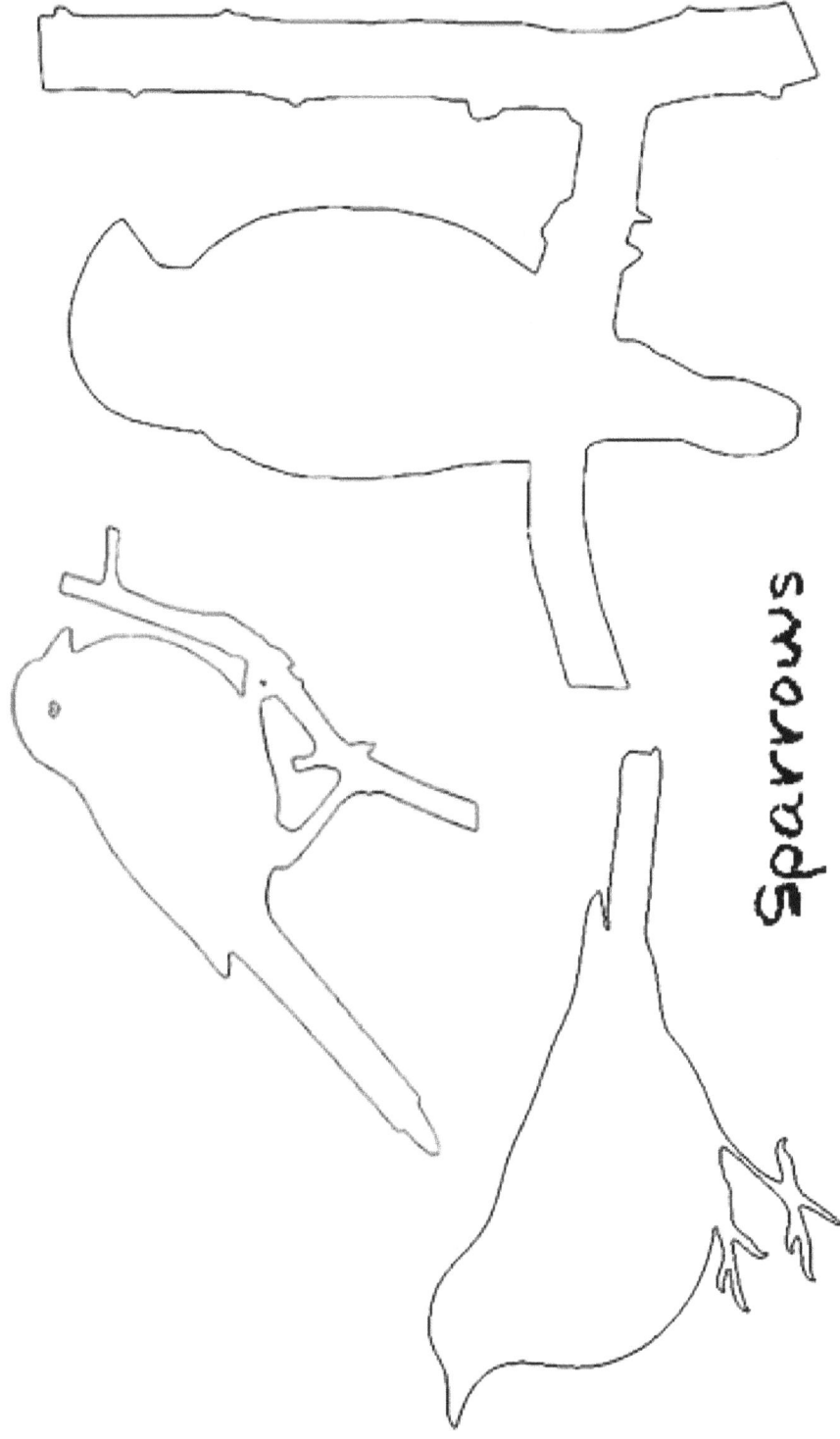

Sparrows

Noah's Ark

TWO AND TWO, MALE AND FEMALE,
WENT INTO THE ARK WITH NOAH, AS
GOD HAD COMMANDED NOAH
GENESIS 7:9

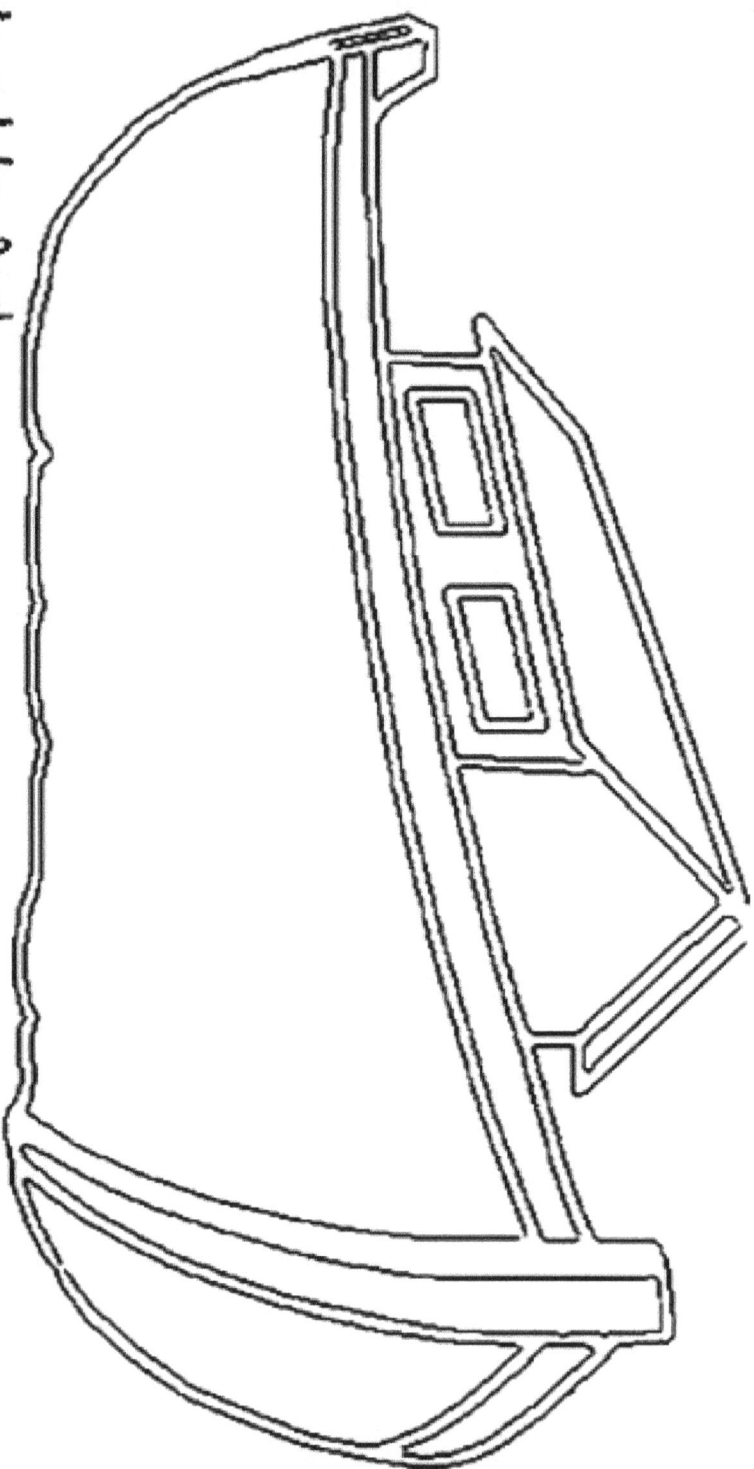

...RISE AND BE BAPTIZED AND WASH AWAY YOUR SINS, CALLING ON HIS NAME
ACTS 22:16

Baby's Baptism

Jesus & Children

YOU SHALL LOVE YOUR NEIGHBOR AS
YOURSELF
MATTHEW 22:39

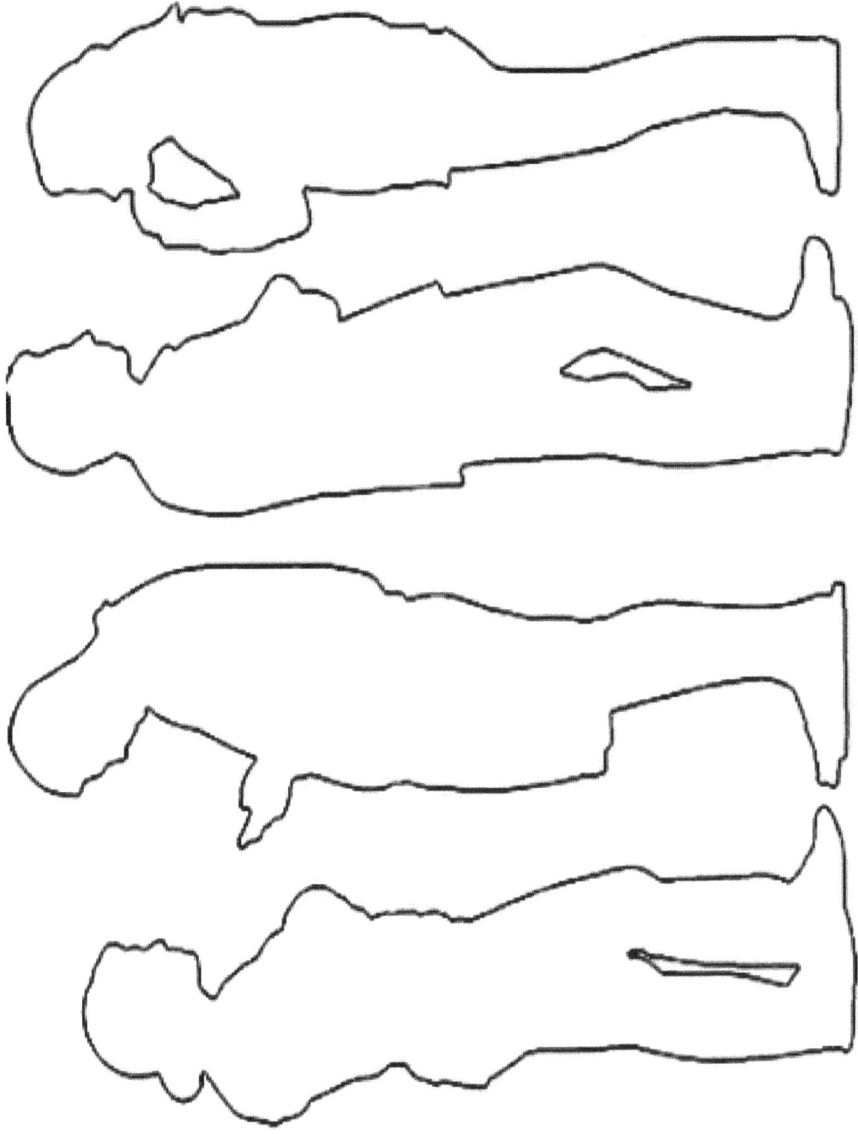

Neighbors

LET THE WORD OF CHRIST DWELL
IN YOU RICHLY
COLOSSIANS 3:16

THE
HOLY BIBLE

OLD AND NEW TESTAMENT

Holy Bible

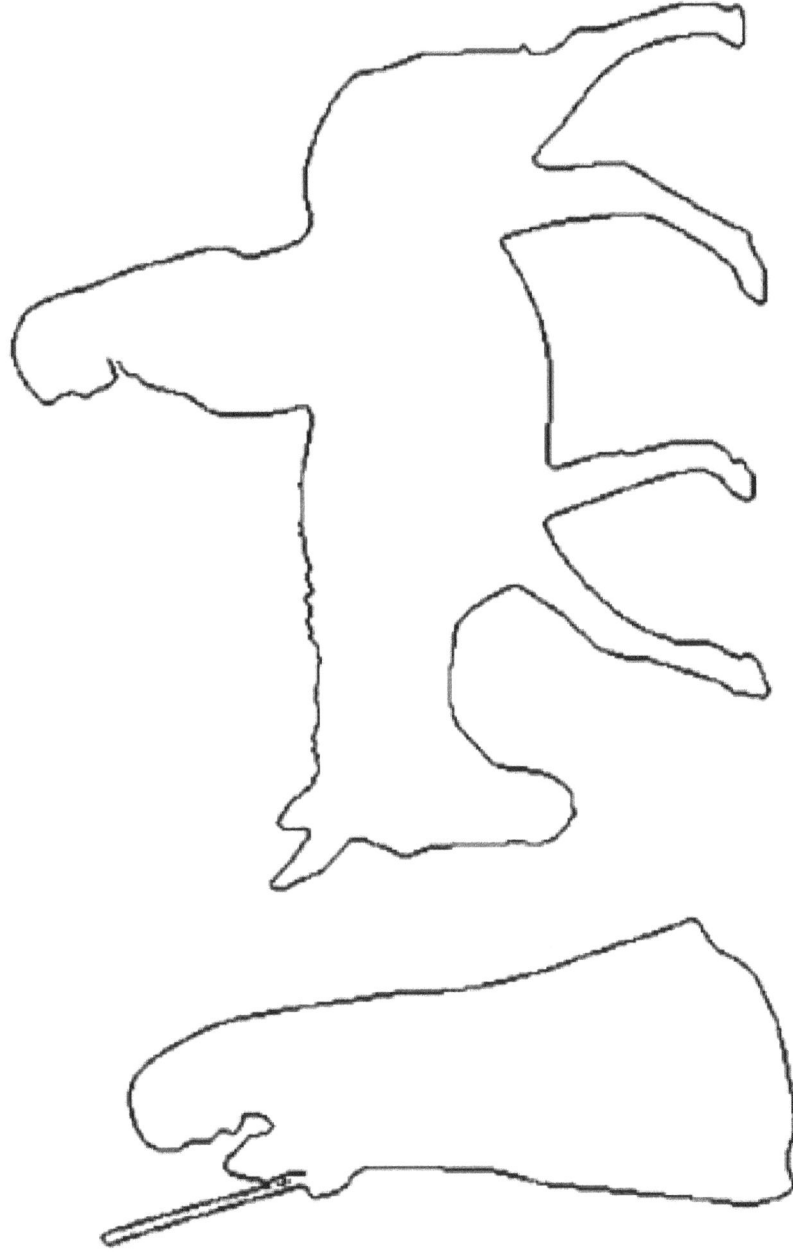

...YOUR KING IS COMING, SITTING ON A
DONKEY'S COLT!...
JOHN 12:12-14

Jesus on Donkey

Jesus Lives

FOR GOD SO LOVED THE WORLD, THAT
HE GAVE HIS ONLY SON...
JOHN 3:16

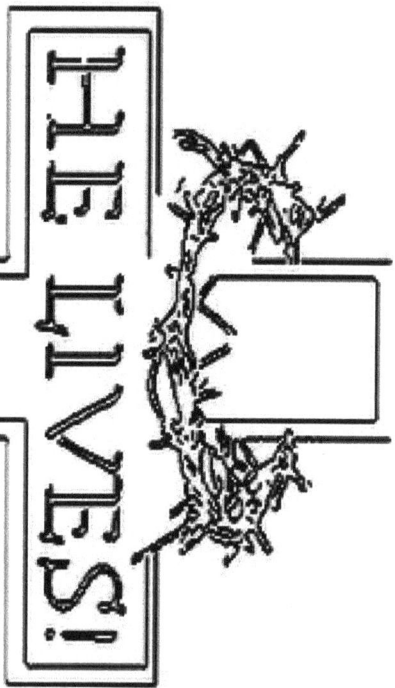

HE LIVES!

AND WITH HIS WOUNDS WE ARE HEALED
ISAIAH 53:4-5

Nails

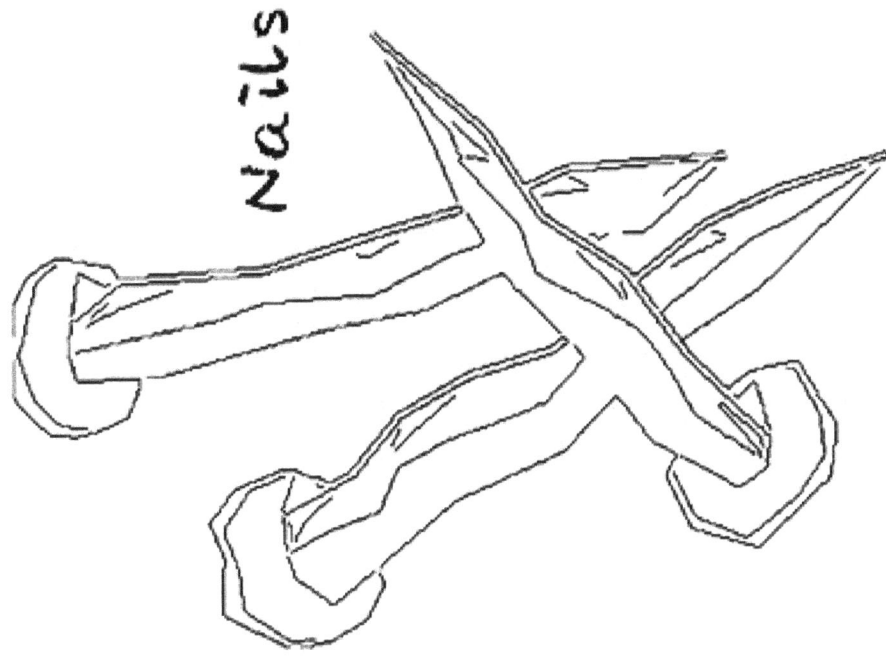

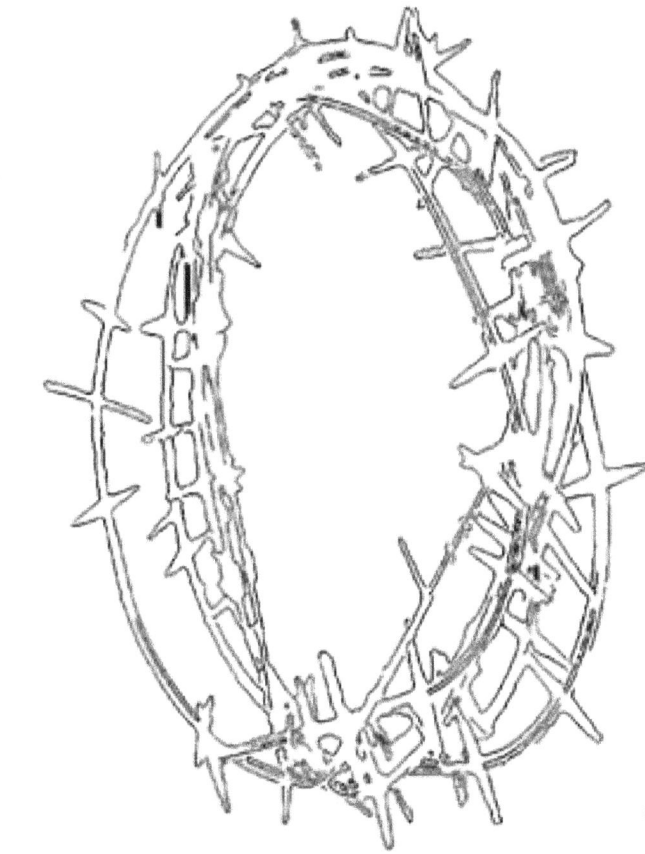

Crown

SO THEY TOOK BRANCHES OF PALM
TREES AND WENT OUT TO MEET HIM
JOHN 12:13

Palm Branch

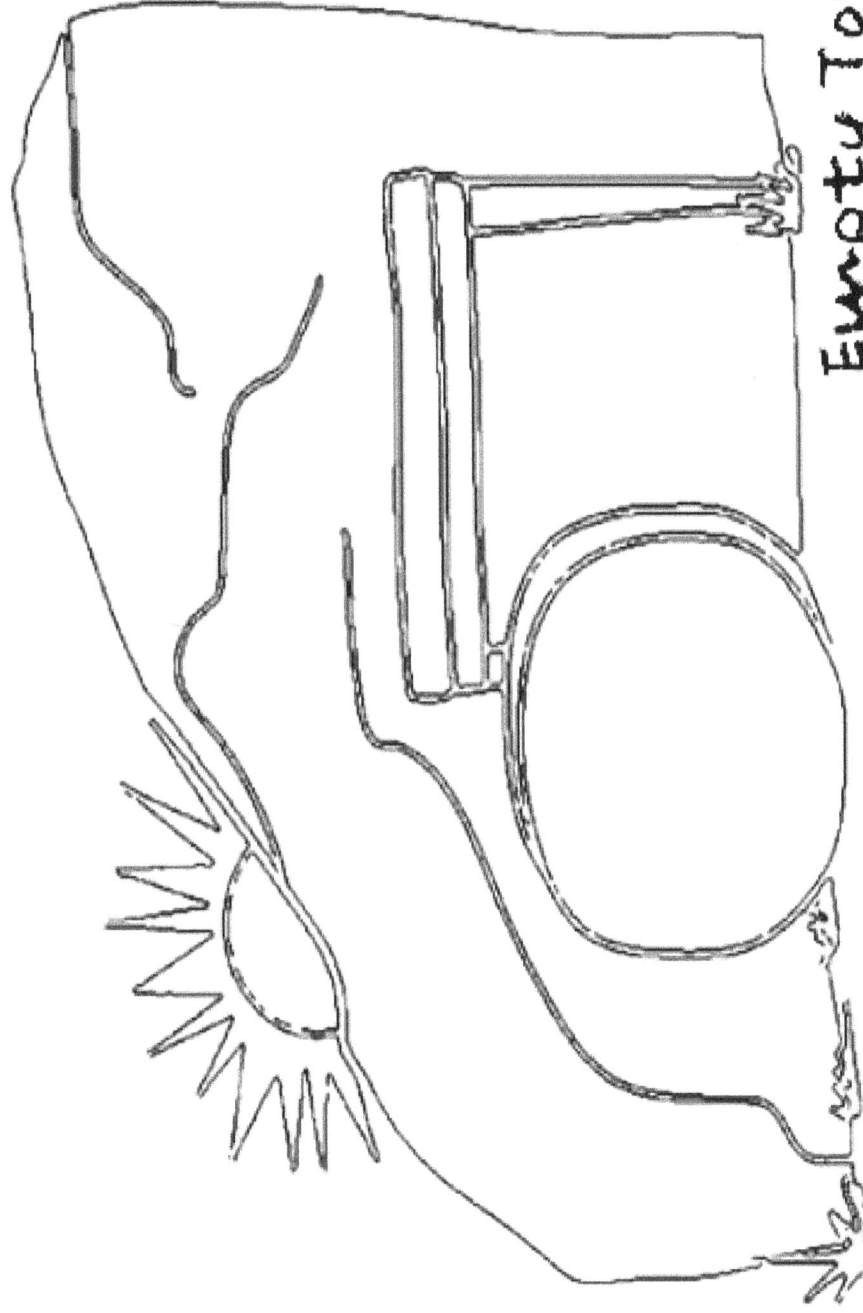

HE IS NOT HERE. HE IS RISEN!
MATTHEW 28:6

Empty Tomb

...THIS IS MY BODY WHICH IS FOR YOU.
DO THIS IN REMEMBRANCE OF ME
I CORINTHIANS 11:24

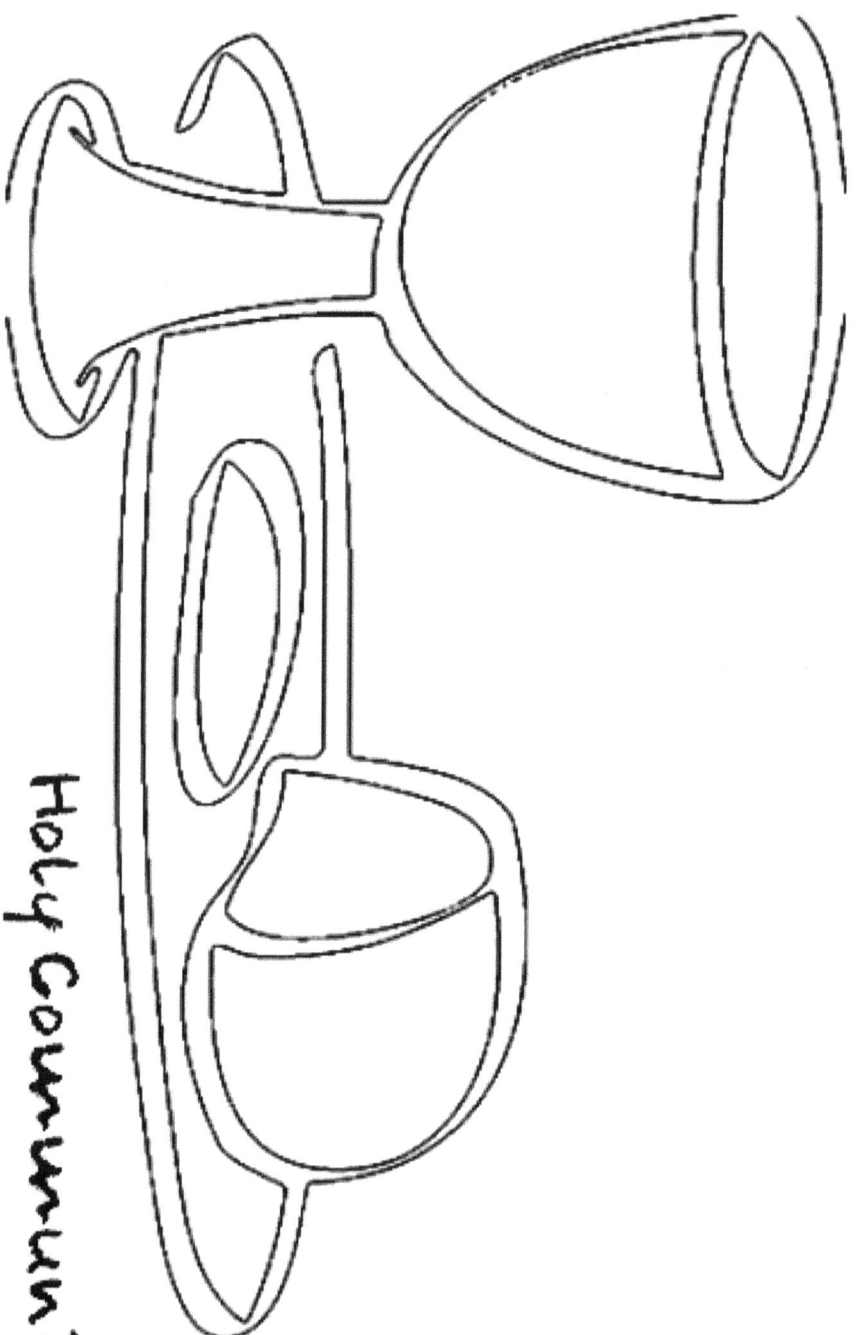

Holy Communion

BUT OF THE TREE OF THE KNOWLEDGE OF GOOD AND EVIL YOU SHALL NOT EAT... GENESIS 2:17

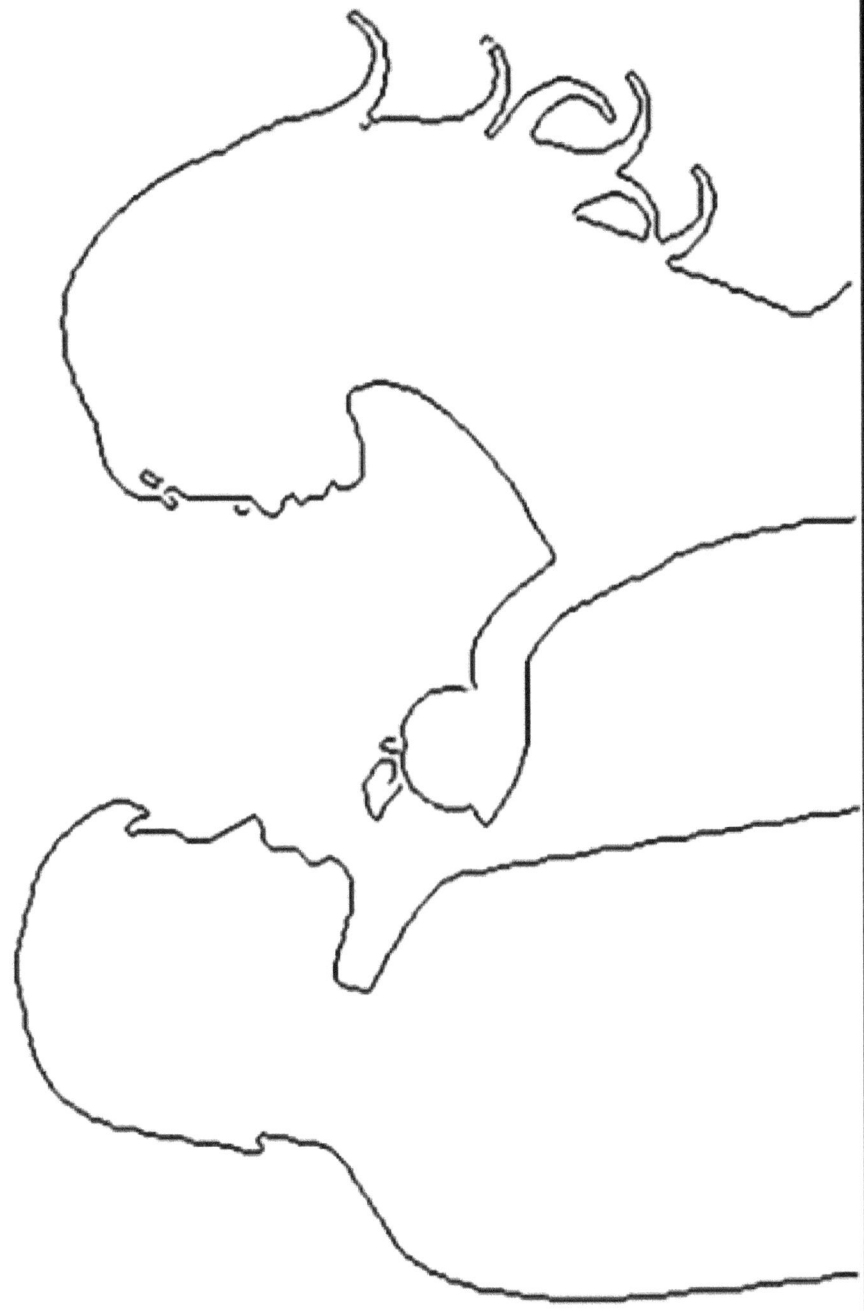

Adam & Eve

Animals

WHOEVER IS RIGHTEOUS HAS REGARD
FOR THE LIFE OF HIS BEAST...
PROVERBS 12:10

OH COME, LET US SING TO THE LORD;
LET US MAKE A JOYFUL NOISE TO THE
ROCK OF OUR SALVATION!
PSALM 95:1-2

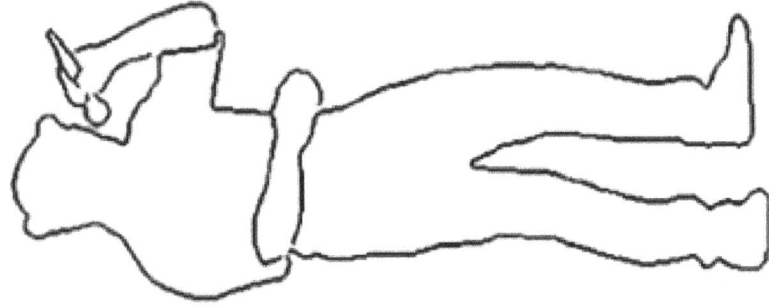

Praise Team

Church

AND I TELL YOU, YOU ARE PETER, AND
ON THIS ROCK I WILL BUILD MY
CHURCH... MATTHEW 16:18

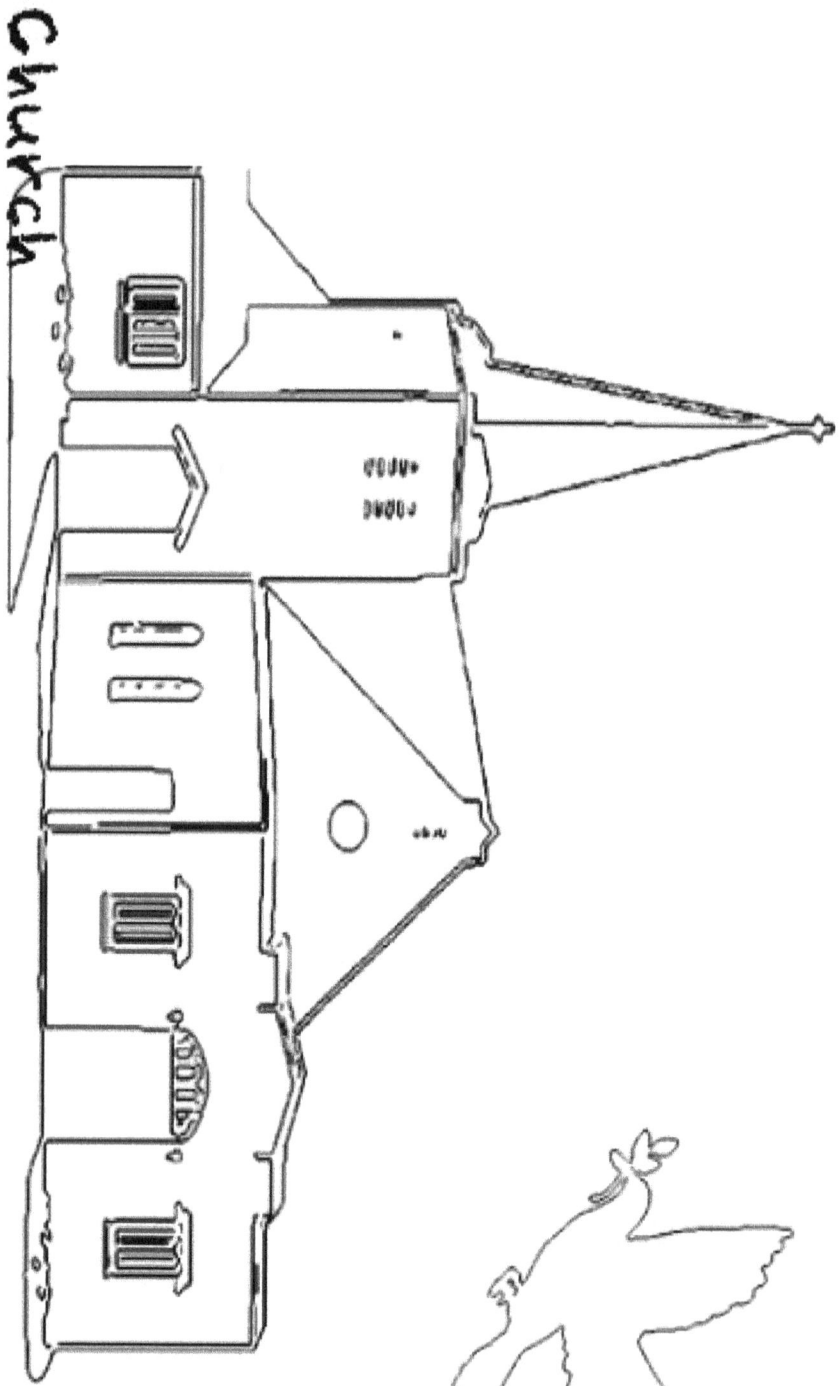

BUT YOU WILL RECEIVE POWER WHEN
THE HOLY SPIRIT HAS COME UPON YOU...
ACTS 1:8

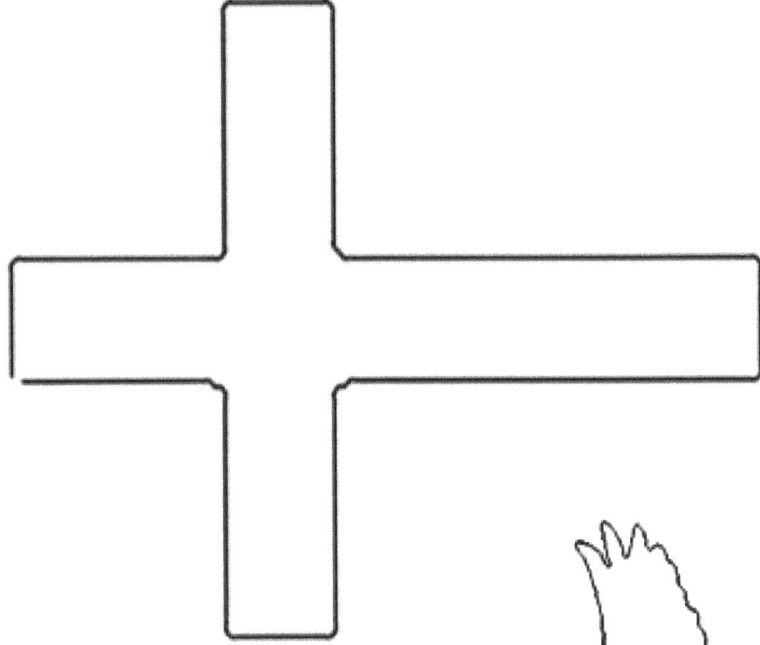

Holy Spirit

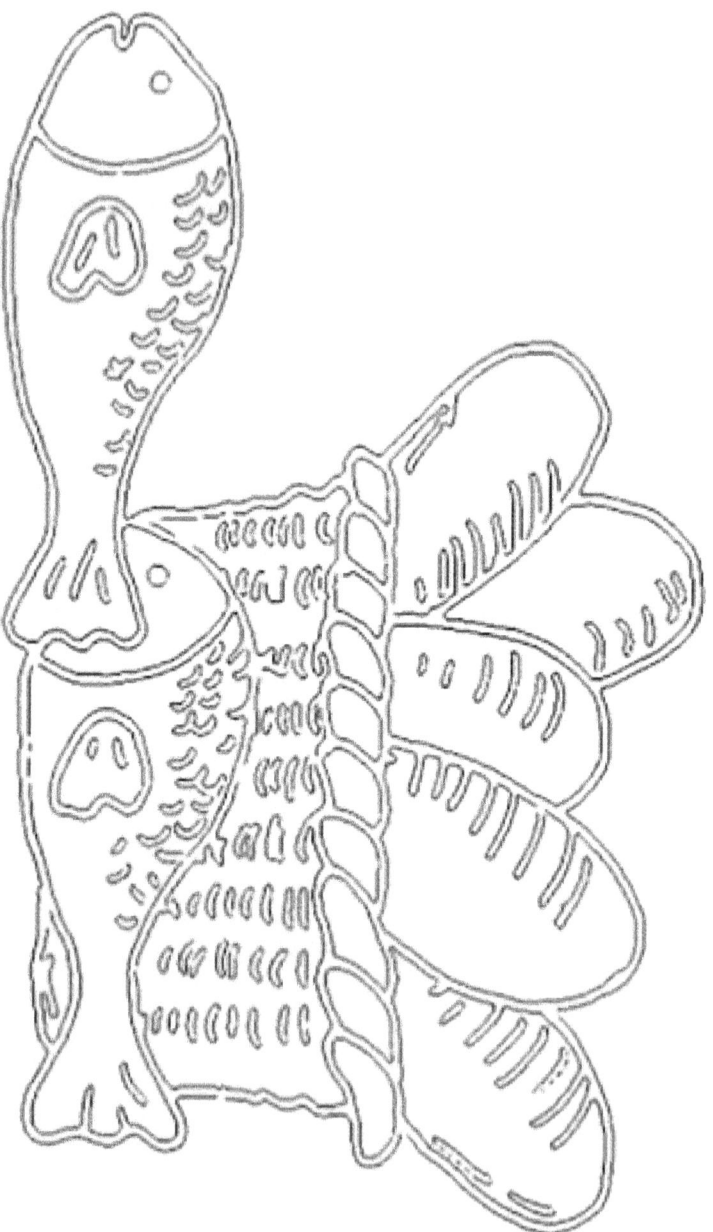

THEY SAID TO HIM, "WE HAVE ONLY FIVE LOAVES HERE AND TWO FISH"...
MATTHEW 14:13-21

Loaves & Fishes

CONTINUE STEADFASTLY IN PRAYER.
BEING WATCHFUL IN IT WITH
THANKSGIVING. COLOSSIANS 4:2

Children Praying

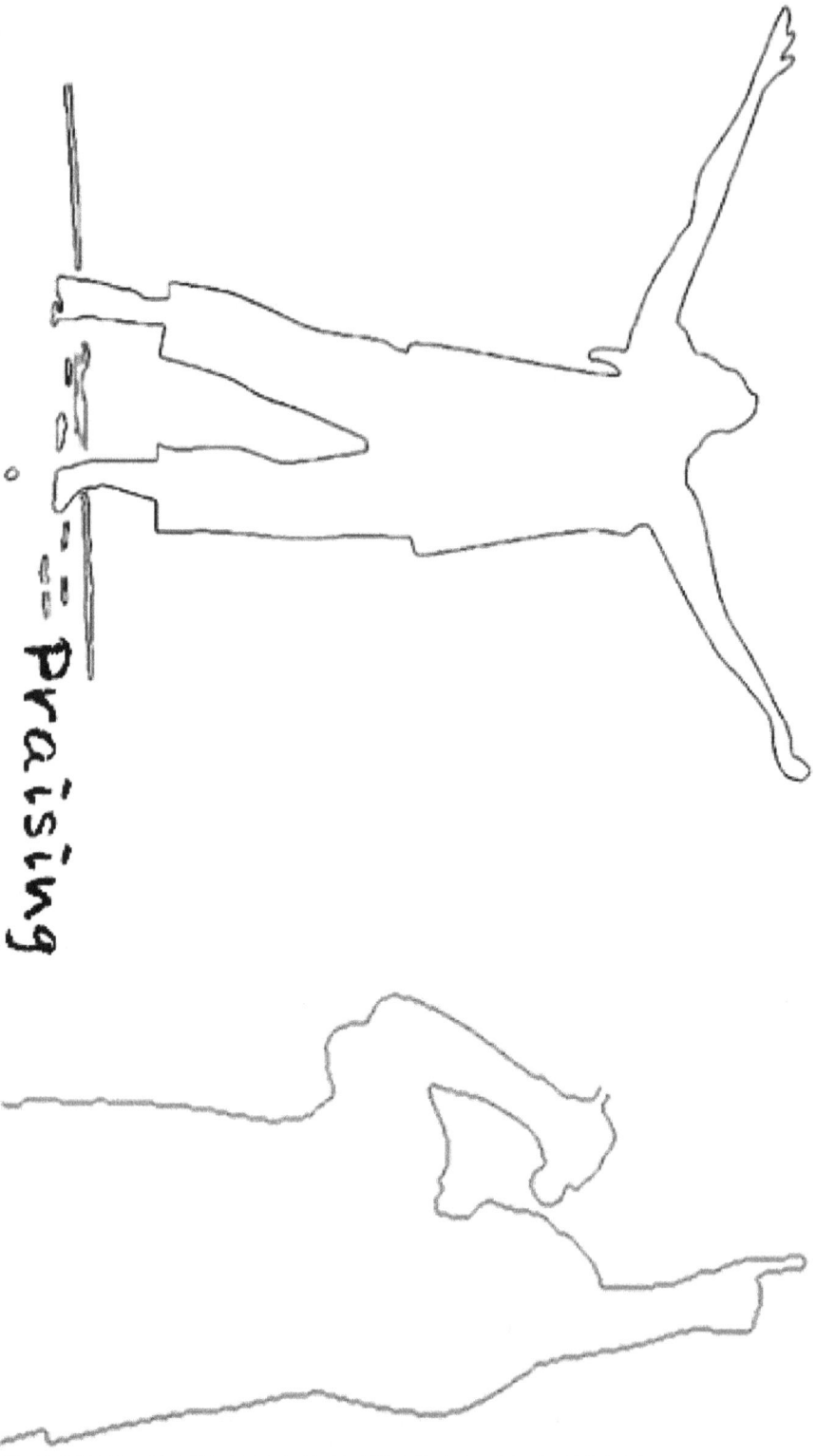

WHATEVER YOU DO, DO EVERYTHING FOR THE GLORY OF GOD
1 CORINTHIANS 10:31

Praising

FOR HE WILL COMMAND HIS ANGELS
CONCERNING YOU TO GUARD YOU IN
ALL YOUR WAYS. PSALM 91:11

Angels Rejoicing

...THEN, OPENING THEIR TREASURES, THEY OFFERED HIM GIFTS, GOLD AND FRANKINCENSE AND MYRRH

MATTHEW 2:11

Three Wise Men

WHEN THEY SAW THE STAR, THEY
REJOICED EXCEEDINGLY WITH GREAT
JOY MATTHEW 2:10

Bethlehem Star

Manger

...BEHOLD, THE VIRGIN SHALL CONCEIVE AND BEAR A SON, AND SHALL CALL HIS NAME IMMANUEL. ISAIAH 7:14

...FOR WE SAW HIS STAR WHEN IT ROSE AND HAVE COME TO WORSHIP HIM

MATTHEW 2:2

Baby Jesus

Ten Commandments

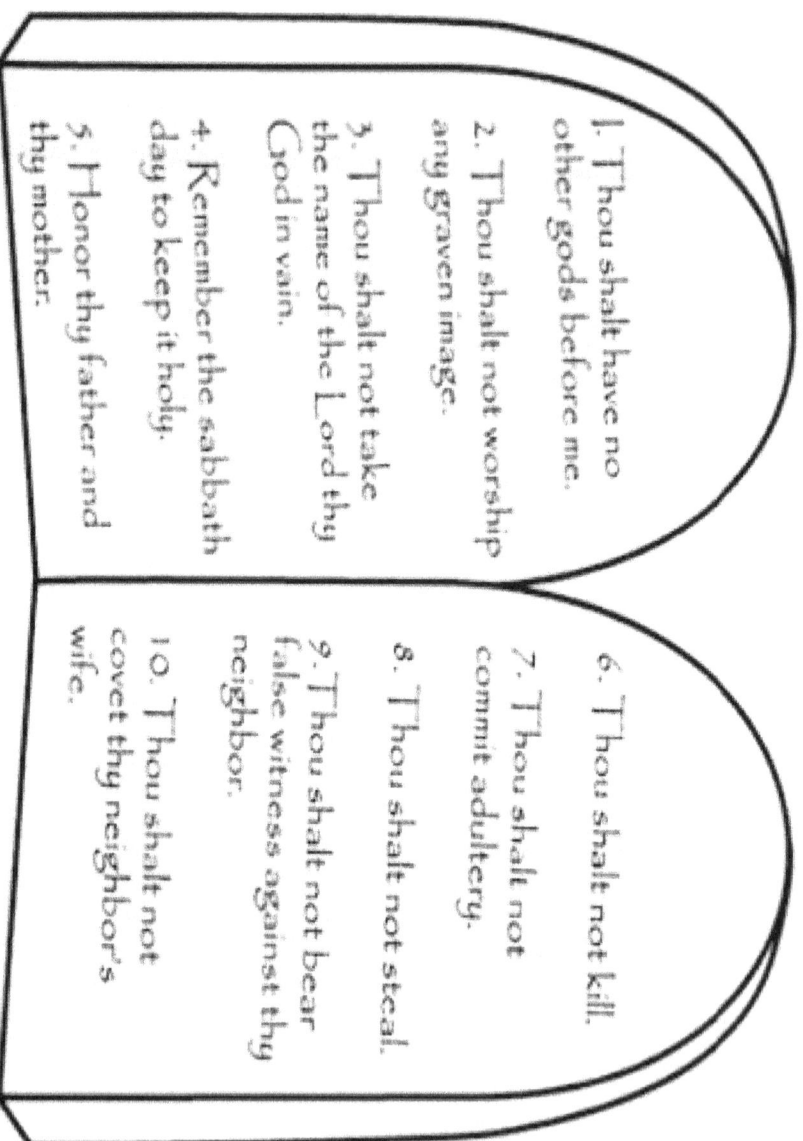

"SO YOU SHALL KEEP MY COMMANDMENTS AND DO THEM: I AM THE LORD." LEVITICUS 22:31

1. Thou shalt have no other gods before me.

2. Thou shalt not worship any graven image.

3. Thou shalt not take the name of the Lord thy God in vain.

4. Remember the sabbath day to keep it holy.

5. Honor thy father and thy mother.

6. Thou shalt not kill.

7. Thou shalt not commit adultery.

8. Thou shalt not steal.

9. Thou shalt not bear false witness against thy neighbor.

10. Thou shalt not covet thy neighbor's wife.

IN THE BEGINNING, GOD
CREATED THE HEAVENS
AND THE EARTH
GENESIS 1:1

THE GRACE OF THE
LORD JESUS BE WITH
GOD'S PEOPLE. AMEN.
REVELATION 22:21

HE IS RISEN INDEED!

WAIT UPON THE LORD!

HOSANNA! HOSANNA!

WISE MEN STILL SEEK HIM!

FOLLOW THE SHINING STAR!

GOD IS GOOD ALL THE TIME!

FOLLOW JESUS CHRIST!

PRAISE THE LORD!

JESUS ROCKS!

GOD'S TIMING IS PERFECT!

HOSANNA IN THE HIGHEST!

TO GOD BE THE GLORY!

CHRIST THE LORD IS RISEN!

PRAISE THE LORD!

IN REMEMBRANCE OF ME

www.ingramcontent.com/pod-product-compliance
Lightning Source LLC
Chambersburg PA
CBHW080947050426
42337CB00055B/4727